Golden Rules for...
Winning Ways by M...

12 Golden Standards

1. Be a good judge of character.
2. Be customer-oriented.
3. Be single-minded.
4. Be captivating in your sales promotion.
5. Be quick to respond.
6. Be vigilant in credit control.
7. Be selective to recruit only the best.
8. Be bold in marketing your product.
9. Be smart in product acquisition.
10. Be adept in analysing marketing opportunities.
11. Be a corporate model.
12. Be farsighted in developing a total business plan.

12 Go...

1. Don't be
2. Don't be
3. Don't be
4. Don't be
5. Don't be
6. Don't sla...
7. Don't giv...
8. Don't wor...
9. Don't be
10. Don't ove...
11. Don't unc... funds str...
12. Don't bli...

Published by ASIAPAC BOOKS PTE LTD 996 Bendemeer Road, #06-08/09 Singapore 339944. Tel: (65) 3928455 Fax

Business Success

aster Tao Zhugong

lden Safeguards

- penny-pinching.
- wishy-washy.
- ostentatious.
- dishonest.
- low in debts collection.
- h prices arbitrarily.
- in to herd instinct.
- against the business cycle.
- a stick-in-the-mud.
- buy on credit.
- er-save — keep reserve
- ng.
- dly endorse a product.

(65) 3926455 E-mail: apacbks@singnet.com.sg Website: www.asiapacbooks.com © All rights reserved.

Asiapac Comics
• STRATEGY & LEADERSHIP •

Golden Rules for Business Success

Winning Ways by Master Tao Zhugong

Illustrated by Fu Chunjiang
Translated by Geraldine Goh & Koh Kok Kiang

ASIAPAC • SINGAPORE

Publisher
ASIAPAC BOOKS PTE LTD
996 Bendemeer Road #06-08/09
Singapore 339944
Tel: (65) 6392 8455
Fax: (65) 6392 6455
Email: asiapacbooks@pacific.net.sg

Visit us at our Internet home page
www.asiapacbooks.com

First published January 1999
2nd edition (revised) November 2000
3rd edition August 2002

© 1999 ASIAPAC BOOKS, SINGAPORE
ISBN 981-229-079-6

All rights reserved. No part of this publication may be reproduced, stored in a retrieval system, or transmitted, in any form or by any means, electronic, mechanical, photocopying, recording, or otherwise, without the prior permission of the publisher. Under no circumstances shall it be rented, resold or redistributed. If this copy is defective, kindly exchange it at the above address.

Cover illustration by Fu Chunjiang
Cover design by Illusion Creative Studio
Body text in Helvetica 8/9pt
Printed in Singapore by Chung Printing

Publisher's Note

It is well-known that the Chinese are good businessmen that can thrive even in the most difficult market conditions. What is the secret of their success?

Golden Rules for Business Success brings to light the success formulas of master enterpreneur Tao Zhugong. It is presented in a light-hearted and easy-to-understand manner for those who want to make their business thrive.

Part of our Strategy & Leadership Series, this book deals specifically with the subject of business management. We hope that it would prove to be useful to businessmen and aspiring entrepreneurs alike.

We are grateful to Mr Soon Peng Yam for his foreword. At the same time, we would like to thank Mr Fu Chunjiang for the artwork, Ms Geraldine Goh and Mr Koh Kok Kiang for the translation, and the production team for putting in their best effort in the publication of this book.

Strategy & Leadership Series in Comics
The Art of Management
The Art of Winning: Wisdom of Tang Tai Zong and Duke Li of Wei
Chinese Business Strategies
Gems of Chinese Wisdom
Golden Rules for Business Success
100 Strategies of War
Sima's Rules of War
Six Strategies for War
Sixteen Strategies of Zhuge Liang
Strategies from the Three Kingdoms
Sun Bin's Art of War
Sunzi's Art of War
Supreme Wisdom: The Art of Insight
Thirty-six Stratagems
Three Strategies of Huang Shi Gong

Foreword

"Chinese Overseas, the greatest entrepreneurs in the world."
(Megatrends Asia by John Naisbitt)

In every part of the world, there is a Chinatown. Chinese businessmen have established a strong financial foundation virtually everywhere they go. They have become the new driving force in the economic network.

The Chinese who left their homes travelled to a foreign land and had to endure great hardships to make a living. Some set up small businesses once they had a little savings. They overcame the language barrier and adapted to a new way of life, running their business based on the traditional code of business ethics and practice. By their perseverance, they succeeded.

Almost every Chinese businessman had his own code of family business practice. Some were passed down by mouth from father to son. Others were recorded like great formulas, framed and hung on the wall. These codes of family business practice are actually quite similar though some may be longer and more detailed. Most of their origins can be traced back to Tao Zhugong.

In China, the name "Tao Zhugong" has become synonymous with a man of great wealth. Thus the proverbial phrase "as rich as Tao Zhugong". But Tao Zhugong was not only admired for his wealth.

Businessmen in the old days also worshipped him as the god of business management. Tao Zhugong left to posterity the secret of his business success. His elements of success included business management techniques, tips to profit-making, and business codes and ethics.

These standard principles were first recorded on bamboo slips and widely circulated among common men. Especially in Tianjin, Suzhou, Ningbo, Hangzhou and Guangzhou, they were faithfully practised and passed down by family businesses from one generation to another.

Through the changing times, the principles were modified. Today, Tao Zhugong's principles of business management is a set of rules that has been revised to perfection. The principles contain the wisdom of generations of successful businessmen. They are referred to as "Tao Zhugong's 12 Steps to Wealth" or "Tao Zhugong's Principles of Business Management". Some businessmen simply call it "The Businessmen's Treasure Trove".

Tao Zhugong's principles are an inward pillar of support to Chinese Overseas businessmen. They are their action compass. A comprehensive study of Tao Zhugong's business techniques reveals that they contain practical tips and advice which are still applicable to today's business organisations. For example, Tao Zhugong's principles teach the entrepreneur to be quick and resourceful to achieve business expansion. A business leader should focus on long-term growth, ensure a balanced account, refrain from overborrowing, choose wisely business areas for development, and above all, persevere.

Tao Zhugong's principles stress on making good use of opportunities. When it is time to act, never procrastinate. Flexibility, too, is important. Read the signs of change and act before changes take place. Be as sensitive as the little creatures who can feel an impending earthquake. Modern-day business techniques, too, have these principles as their foundation.

In this light, Tao Zhugong can be regarded as not only a great economist, but also a genius in business and commerce. And he rightly deserves the accolade. Indeed, Tao Zhugong, the authority of ancient Chinese economic theory, is aptly lauded as the founding father of the Chinese business school of thought.

Asiapac Books has approached me to write the foreword for Tao Zhugong's Principles of Business Management which has been reproduced in comics that is easy to read and understand. It is a meaningful effort and I am very pleased to recommend this great book which light-heartedly portrays the wit and wisdom of Tao Zhugong. Compare these principles to your own management techniques and you will be greatly enlightened.

Soon Peng Yam
December 22, 1998

Soon Peng Yam is the founder and adviser of Sim Lim Co (Pte) Ltd. For over thirty years, he has been the chairman of the Ee Hoe Hean Club, the Chinese Swimming Club, and the Tung Ann District Guild in Singapore. He is also the Honorary President of the Singapore Chinese Chamber of Commerce & Industry.

Related Titles

Fan Li & Xi Shi: Master Strategist and the Beauty
Fan Li, also known as Tao Zhugong, was a political, military and business genius. Discover the life and thoughts of the strategist.

Tao Zhugong is also well known among Chinese merchants. In fact, he is revered as God of Wealth. This book will tell you more.

Chinese Ways to Wealth
(Comics by Jeffrey Seow)
This book provides an understanding into the Chinese outlook and mindset on wealth. It traces the origins of some of the most revered Chinese gods and how they evolve to become gods of wealth worshipped by the masses.

Besides Tao Zhugong's business formula, you can discover the success secret of other Chinese entrepreneurs!

Chinese Business Strategies
(Comics by Ma Weichi)
The secret of Chinese business success lies in 10 time-tested principles of entrepreneurship. The book offers readers 30 real life case studies with comments on their application.

About the Illustrator

Fu Chunjiang, born in 1974, is a native of Chongqing municipality in southeastern China's Sichuan province. He has been fond of drawing ever since childhood and graduated in Chinese language studies. Fu loves traditional Chinese culture and has tried his hand at drawing comics.

Since 1994 he has been drawing comics and his works include *The Story of Kites* and *The Faint-Hearted Hero*. He has also participated in the production of *One Riddle For One Story*.

His comics entitled *Origins of Chinese Festivals* and *The Chinese Code of Success: Maxims by Zhu Zi* published by Asiapac Books have been widely acclaimed.

Characters in this book

Master Tao Zhugong
Founder and Director of Tao Enterprises. Also known as Tao Gong, he guides his three sons in running the businesses that he has set up at Dingtao. Has his own set of rules for business success and is immensely rich.

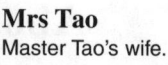

Mrs Tao
Master Tao's wife.

Kang Bao Medical Hall

Tao Zizhang
Master Tao's eldest son. Trained by his father in business management since he was a boy and holds a position equivalent to today's General Manager in Tao Merchandise.

Uncle He
Manager of Kang Bao Medical Hall, the medicine shop of Tao Enterprises.

Tao Zici
Wholesales Manager of Tao Merchandise.

Uncle Zhao
He keeps the books for Tao Merchandise. In charge of money matters, he is equivalent to today's Finance Manager.

Uncle De
Pharmacist of Kang Bao Medical Hall.

Tao Zixiao
Retail Manager of Tao Merchandise.

Uncle Chen
Chief Purchaser of Tao Merchandise.

Xiaowen
Employee of Kang Bao Medical Hall.

Ah Mu
Employee of Tao Merchandise.

Ah He
Employee of Tao Merchandise.

Zheng Huaishan
Proprietor of established medicine shop, Huai Shan Medical Hall, which sells a wide range of Chinese herbs and medicines.

Uncle Fa
Manager of Huai Shan Hall, he assists Zheng Huaishan in running his medicine shop.

Xiao Shengli
Proprietor of Sheng Li Medical Hall which sells a wide range of Chinese herbs and medicines.

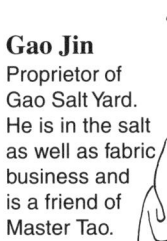

Gao Jin
Proprietor of Gao Salt Yard. He is in the salt as well as fabric business and is a friend of Master Tao.

Gao Zheng
Gao Jin's son and proprietor of Gao Textile Store.

Lingqiu Zi
Manager of Lingqiu Bee Farm. The bee farm is a family business. His father and Master Tao are friends.

Tiancai
Proprietor of Ji Bao Jewellery Store, he specialises in the jewellery trade.

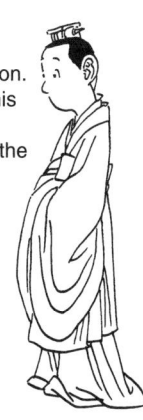

Xiaocai
Tiancai's son. He helps his father in managing the jewellery business.

Contents

Tao Zhugong   *1*

12 Golden Standards

1. Be a good judge of character.   *9*

2. Be customer-oriented.   *19*

3. Be single-minded.   *29*

4. Be captivating in your sales promotion.   *41*

5. Be quick to respond.   *51*

6. Be vigilant in credit control.   *59*

7. Be selective to recruit only the best.   *67*

8. Be bold in marketing your product.   *75*

9. Be smart in product acquisition.   *83*

10. Be adept in analysing marketing opportunities.   *91*

11. Be a corporate model.   *99*

12. Be farsighted in developing a total business plan.   *107*

12 Golden Safeguards

1.	Don't be penny-pinching.	*115*
2.	Don't be wishy-washy.	*123*
3.	Don't be ostentatious.	*131*
4.	Don't be dishonest.	*139*
5.	Don't be slow in debts collection.	*147*
6.	Don't slash prices arbitrarily.	*155*
7.	Don't give in to herd instinct.	*163*
8.	Don't work against the business cycle.	*171*
9.	Don't be a stick-in-the-mud.	*179*
10.	Don't overbuy on credit.	*187*
11.	Don't under-save — keep reserve funds strong.	*195*
12.	Don't blindly endorse a product.	*203*

Tao Zhugong, also known as Fan Li, lived during the Spring and Autumn Period. He was a native of Wan (Nanyang, Henan Province) in the state of Chu.

Fighting broke out between the states of Yue and Wu at Huiji. When Yue lost the battle, the Lord of Yue, Goujian, became a slave at Wu.

As an official serving Goujian, Fan Li left with him for Wu. With his brilliant planning, Goujian's return to Yue became a reality.

Fan Li and Wen Zhong (another loyal official) assisted Goujian. After 10 years of suffering, Goujian had his revenge and destroyed Wu.

能识人　知人善恶　帐目不负
néng shī rén　zhī rén shàn è　zhàng mù bú fù

BE A GOOD JUDGE OF CHARACTER.

In work involving buying and selling, accounting and making loans, it is important that one deals with a party who can be trusted — the principle of "personal guarantee". This involves making a judgement on who may be trusted based on the person's words, demeanour, actions and background. In this way, one can avoid damage and loss caused by untrustworthy people.

能结纳 礼文相待 交关者众
néng jiē nà   lǐ wén xiāng dài   jiāo guān zhě zhòng

BE CUSTOMER-ORIENTED.

In modern terms, providing good service will bring about customer satisfaction. This includes good product knowledge, customer relations and sales techniques. In addition, modern practices such as hire purchase, after-sales service and prompt delivery have become an integral part of good service. Beyond that, the right attitude towards providing good service is crucial to business development.

能 安 业　厌 故 喜 新　商 贾 大 病
néng ān yè　yàn gù xǐ xīn　shāng gǔ dà bìng

BE SINGLE-MINDED.

Sincerity is an essential trait for any business venture. Besides, one must be knowledgeable and be prepared to work and study to become an expert in the field. Only in this way can one gain a foothold in the market and succeed.

Lingqiu Zi took over his father's business in rearing bees.

In bee-keeping, one must constantly check the beehives. If two queen bees are found, they have to be kept apart.

Then one has to always get rid of pests such as ants and spiders.

When collecting honey, one has to leave behind a sufficient quantity as food for the bees.

Aiyah! It's tough keeping bees.

Hence Lingqiu Zi used the proceeds from the sale of the apiary to start a tree plantation.

He employed people to plant, water and take care of the seedlings.

As the seedlings required 10 years to mature, it was not possible to reap immediate harvests.

Although Lingqiu Zi owned a large plantation, he could not derive any benefit from it.

There's hardly any growth.

He watched his investment carefully but to no avail.

能 整 顿　货 物 整 齐　夺 人 心 目
néng zhěng dùn　huò wù zhěng qí　dúo rén xīn mù

BE CAPTIVATING IN YOUR SALES PROMOTION.

Reorganising, revamping or restructuring is a science of management. It covers all aspects of an organization — image, marketing, income, human resource, company culture, work attitude, etc. Only by constant restructuring can a business keep up with the times.

能 敏 捷　犹 豫 不 决　终 归 无 成
néng mǐn jié　yóu yù bù jué　zhōng guī wú chéng

BE QUICK TO RESPOND.

The business world is like a battlefield. In a battle, the adroit soldier wins. In business, the resourceful entrepreneur who meets demands timely succeeds. All this boils down to seizing the opportunity when it knocks. Lack of confidence, fear of taking risks and a weak mind are reasons for failure to act. The guiding principle is to provide needed goods and services. If this is heeded, profits will roll in.

䏻 讨 帐　　勤 谨 不 怠　　取 讨 自 多
néng tǎo zhàng　qín jǐn bú dài　qǔ tǎo zì duō

BE VIGILANT IN CREDIT CONTROL.

Pressing clients for settlement of accounts is a difficult and thankless task. Unlike sales, there is no glamour in the job. But the work has to be done to minimise bad debts and to maintain a balance in receipts and expenditure. If no one wishes to undertake the task, the boss himself should take charge.

Master Tao's eldest son, Tao Zizhang, was the manager of Tao Merchandise.

Tao Merchandise was into both retailing and wholesaling.

The distribution network in wholesaling was wider and credit was often extended to customers. There would be accounts still unsettled when books were due to be closed at the end of the year.

Uncle Zhao, let's discuss how we should go about asking for payments.

All right.

舡 用 人　因 才 器 使　任 事 有 赖
néng yòng rén　yīn cái qì shǐ　rèn shì yǒu lài

BE SELECTIVE TO RECRUIT ONLY THE BEST.

The success of an enterprise depends on the quality of its staff. This in turn depends on the recruitment, management and training of staff. To deploy staff effectively, one has to know their aptitudes and talents, give them room for growth and not interfere too much with their work.

能 辩 论　坐 财 有 道　阐 发 愚 蒙
néng biàn lùn　zuò cái yǒu dào　chǎn fā yú méng

BE BOLD IN MARKETING YOUR PRODUCT.

There is a proverb: "Old Woman Wang sells gourds; she praises what she sells." It has a derogatory connotation. However, in promoting good things, one must bear in mind the saying: "When the stuff is good, don't be tongue-tied." Hence if a business person is able to act according to the right principles, earn the trust of customers, and help them to appreciate the value of his products so as to be able to make a sale, it can be said to be a positive form of the "Old Woman Wang spirit".

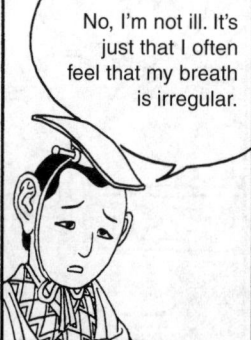

能办货　置货不苛　蚀本便经
néng bàn huò　zhí huò bù kē　shí běn biàn jīng

BE SMART IN PRODUCT ACQUISITION.

Cheap stuff may not be quality goods; those who are eager to sell do not have genuine things. When selecting goods, one must be meticulous in inspecting things and not order casually, otherwise one would incur a loss. Likewise, when taking delivery of goods, one must be as thorough in checking them.

Remember: Be thorough and meticulous when stocking up to ensure high turnover.

能 知 机　售 贮 随 时　可 称 名 哲
néng zhī jī　shòu zhù suí shí　kě chēng míng zhé

BE ADEPT IN ANALYSING MARKETING OPPORTUNITIES.

There are two aspects to making business plans. One is the effect of natural factors on the quantity produced, and the other is the effect of demand and supply. Scarce or bountiful supply will determine if prices are high or low. Similarly, strong or weak demand will determine whether prices will rise or fall.

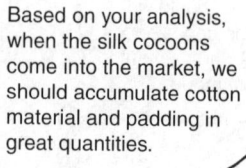

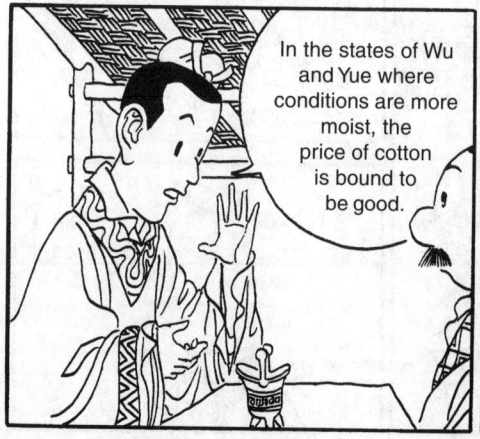

能倡率　躬行以律　亲感自生
néng chàng shuài　gōng xíng yǐ lù　qīn gǎn zì shēng

BE A CORPORATE MODEL.

Taking the lead to embrace the enterprise's corporate culture or business principles is one of the factors of success for the leader. This not only promotes trust and a sense of togetherness between superiors and subordinates, but also helps improve staff relations.

能远数　多寡宽紧　酌中而行
néng yuǎn shù　duō guǎ kuān jǐn　zhuó zhōng ér xíng

BE FARSIGHTED IN DEVELOPING A TOTAL BUSINESS PLAN.

Foresight and the ability to read a situation accurately are essential in making investment plans. Blind investments will result in financial losses. Planning ahead means being sensitive to market changes. Policies can only be effectively implemented when market trends are recognised.

勿 卑 陋　应 纳 无 文　交 关 不 至
wù bēi lòu　yìng nà wú wén　jiāo guān bú zhì

DON'T BE PENNY-PINCHING.

A niggardly businessman paints an unflattering picture of himself and is shunned. Donating to disaster funds and sharing the costs of public projects like building bridges and road repairs are ways to serve the society. Socialising and doing charity work are part and parcel of public relations. One's status and reputation can be elevated through these activities. In turn, this creates opportunities for widening the scope of the business.

勿优柔 胸无果敢 经营不振
wù yōu róu xiōng wú guǒ gǎn jīng yíng bú zhèn

DON'T BE WISHY-WASHY.

Failure to act at the opportune moment results in lost opportunities for business expansion. Time is wasted when efforts put in are not followed up and business stagnates. It is a pitfall which business leaders must avoid.

Remember: Lack of resolution results in business stagnation.

勿 虚 华　用 度 不 节　破 败 之 端
wù xū huá　yòng dù bù jié　pò bài zhī duān

DON'T BE OSTENTATIOUS.

Businesspeople value thrift and avoid extravagance. Traditional Chinese companies begin as small family concerns. A family keeps spending at a basic level and thrift is stressed. In modern business practice, it is wrong to overspend and to borrow heavily to satisfy one's vanity. Irreparable damage is done when huge losses incurred cannot be recouped.

勿强辩　暴心待人　祸患难免
wù qiáng biàn　bào xīn dài rén　huò huàn nán miǎn

DON'T BE DISHONEST.

In the olden days, profiteers cheated by selling fake medicines and wines. Today, illegal practices have 'evolved' into infringing copyrights and stealing trade secrets. There are rules in market competition, the first and foremost being fairness. Infringement of rights and stealing are illegal and will not be tolerated by the law.

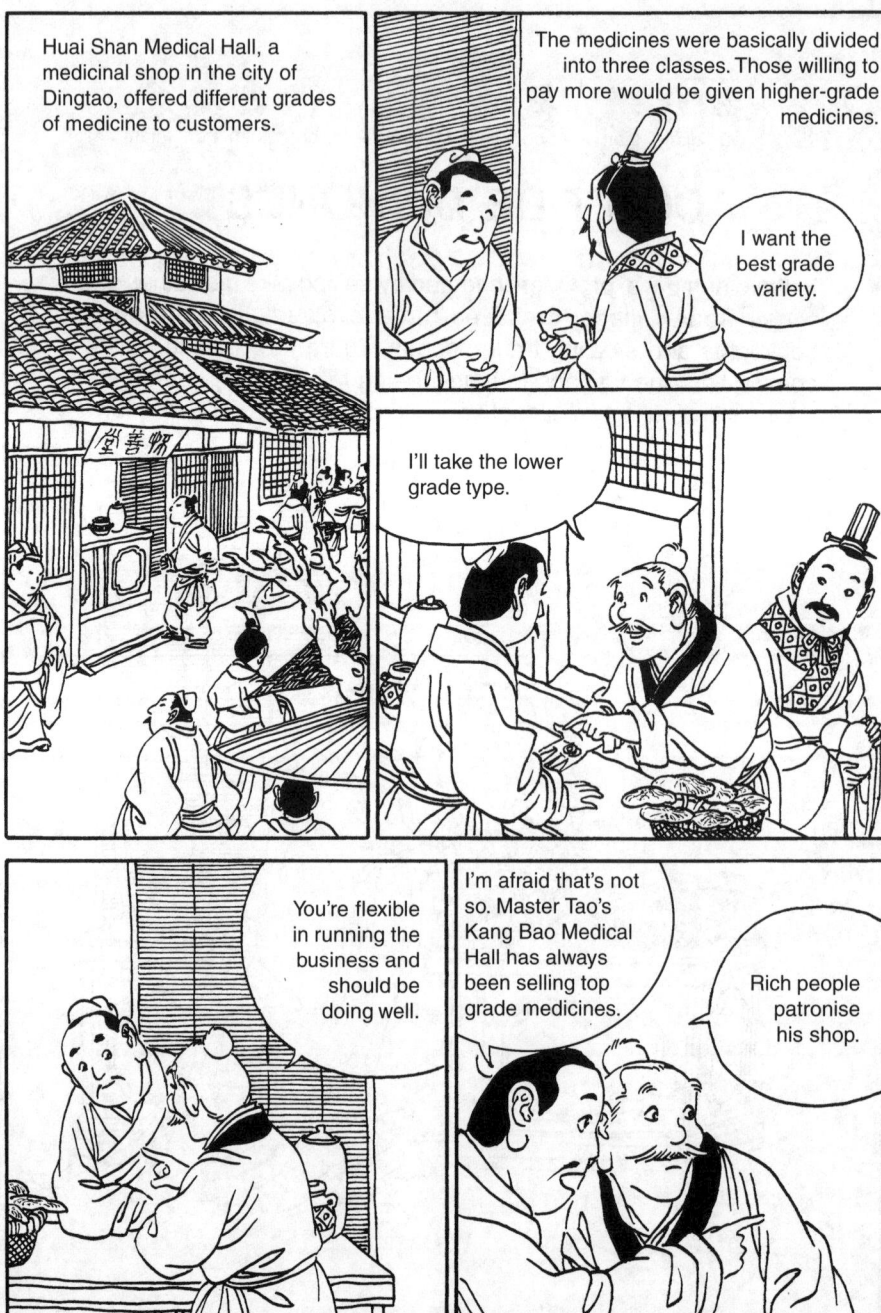

勿懒惰　取讨不力　帐目无有
wù lǎn duò　qǔ tǎo bú lì　zhàng mù wú yǒu

DON'T BE SLOW IN DEBTS COLLECTION.

Collecting payment is the last stage of a sale process. A sale is deemed to be successful only when payment is made. At times, a battle of strength of character between the creditor and debtor ensues. Some rely on goodwill to defend their position or launch an attack. When pressing for payment, one should stay positive and never give up.

勿 轻 出　货 物 轻 出　血 本 必 亏
wù qīng chū　huò wù qīng chū　xuě běn bì kuī

DON'T SLASH PRICES ARBITRARILY.

Violent price fluctuations result when competitors try to outdo each other by raising and slashing prices. Ultimately, the business suffers. Set prices at a level which consumers are comfortable with. This helps the business to gain a firm foothold in the market and profits are maximised.

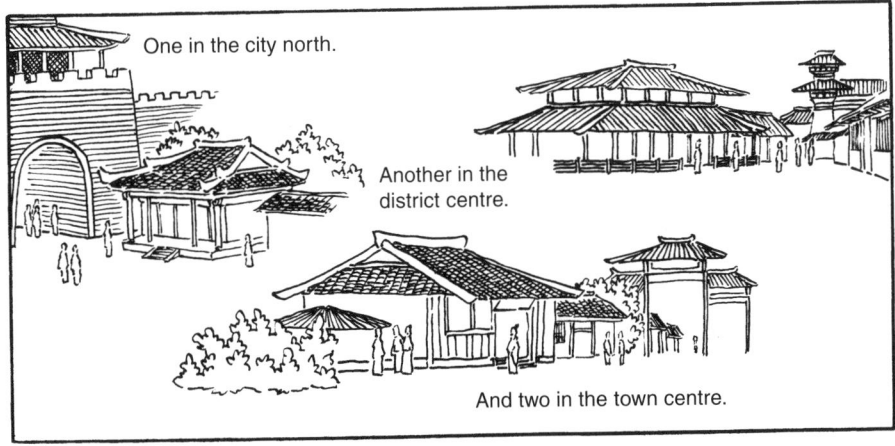

Remember:
Design pricing strategies to meet sales margin.

勿 争 取　货 重 争 趋　需 防 跌 价
wù zhēng qǔ　huò zhòng zhēng qū　xū fáng diē jià

DON'T GIVE IN TO HERD INSTINCT.

Prices fall when they reach the ceiling but rise when the bottom is hit. This is how market forces work. To simply follow the trend and sell what others are selling gives the businessman little flexibility in responding to changing demands. In consequence, losses occur.

勿 昧 时　依 时 贮 发　各 有 常 道
wù mèi shí　yī shí zhù fā　gè yǒu cháng dào

DON'T WORK AGAINST THE BUSINESS CYCLE.

Timeliness is important in business. An entrepreneur has to be able to adapt to changes so that opportunities would not be lost. He must possess the ability to make accurate forecasts not only on product supply but also market demand and price changes.

勿 固 执　拘 执 不 通　便 成 枯 木
wù gù zhí　jū zhí bù tōng　biàn chéng kū mù

DON'T BE A STICK-IN-THE-MUD.

When one is conservative and stubborn, the business suffers. By rejecting good ideas and new techniques, the business cannot prosper and will lose its viability.

Huai Shan Medical Hall was the most well-known medicine shop in Dingtao.

It carried a good range of medicines. The medicines were divided into different grades and priced accordingly. Both the poor and the rich became regular patrons of the shop. Business had always been good.

One day, when the proprietor and the chief shopkeeper were doing the accounts ...

Uncle Fa, what is our profit this month?

勿 贪 赊　贪 赊 多 估　承 卖 莫 续
wù tān shē　tān shē duō gū　chéng mài mò xù

DON'T OVERBUY ON CREDIT.

It is easy to pay for purchases by credit card but remember the risk of overspending. It is also easy to obtain credit for the business but always be wary of hidden snares. The recent turmoil in the Asian economy is mainly a consequence of overborrowing.

A few days into the journey, there was a storm. Pieces of the pottery were broken.

I'll have to turn to selling jewellery and jade items to recoup my losses. The profits are better.

He set off for Qi with gems and jewellery worth 500 pieces of gold.

Xiaocai sought Zici's help again. He needed to buy on credit.

勿 薄 蓄　货 贱 则 积　恢 复 必 速
wù báo xù　huò jiàn zé jī　huī fù bì sù

DON'T UNDER-SAVE —
KEEP RESERVE FUNDS STRONG.

When prices hit rock bottom, the only direction they can go is up. The big winners are those with ready cash at hand. Reserve funds and skills development are both essential in building up a business.

Three months later, Qi troops returned victorious.

Master Tao sold the five chests of jewels at Qi.

With the profits he made, he bought three cargo boats. With the cargo boats, Master Tao did not have to rely solely on land transport to carry his goods.

Remember: High reserves enable you to stock up goods when prices are low.

勿 痴 货　优 劣 不 分　遗 害 非 浅
wù chī huò　yōu liè bù fēn　yí hài fēi qiǎn

DON'T BLINDLY ENDORSE A PRODUCT.

Pay more for quality but even then, one may sometimes be disappointed. When the quality of the favoured brand does not measure up to expectations, one would be forced to sell below the cost price. In today's business world where the market is flooded with big labels, caution should be exercised.

CHINESE CULTURE SERIES
Capture the essence of Chinese culture in comics

Title	*Price S$	Qty	Total
Origins of Chinese Festivals	$14.30		
Origins of Chinese Cuisine	$14.30		
Origins of Chinese People and Customs	$7.70		
Origins of Chinese Music and Art	$7.70		
Origins of Chinese Folk Arts	$7.70		
Origins of Chinese Martial Arts	$7.70		
Origins of Chinese Food and Drinks (forthcoming)	$7.70		
Origins of Chinese Medicine (forthcoming)	$7.70		

* *Nett prices indicated after discount (GST incl.). Free postage for Singapore only.*
Note: For overseas orders, please include postage fees:
Surface mail: S$5.00 for every book.
Air mail: S$8.00 for every book.

I wish to purchase the above-mentioned titles at the nett price of S$ _____
Enclosed is my postal order/money order/cheque for S$_____ (No.: _____)
Name (Mr/Mrs/Ms) _____ Tel _____
Address_____
_____ Fax _____
Please charge the amount of S$ _____ to my VISA/MASTER CARD account
(only Visa/Master Card accepted)
Card No. _____ Card Expiry Date _____

Card Holder's Name _____ Signature _____

Send to:
ASIAPAC BOOKS PTE LTD
996 Bendemeer Road #06-09 Singapore 339944 Tel: (65)63928455 Fax: (65)63926455
E-mail: asiapacbooks@pacific.net.sg   Website: www.asiapacbooks.com
Note: Prices include GST and are valid for purchase by mail order only. Prices subject to change without prior notice.

Asiapac Website

Visit us at our Internet home page for more information on Asiapac titles.

Asiapac Books Homepage
www.asiapacbooks.com

You will find:
- Asiapac — The Company
- Asiapac Logo
- Asiapac Publications
- Comics Extracts
- Book Reviews
- New Publications
- Ordering Our Publications

Or drop us a line at:
sales@asiapacbooks.com *(for ordering books)*
asiapacbooks@pacific.net.sg *(for general correspondence)*

经商宝典

编写：徐晖

绘画：傅春江

翻译：吴杰欣、许国强

 亚太图书有限公司出版